When I entered the large auditorium, it was packed with people.

Loud cheers came from the black section of the audience, and fainter cheers from some whites. . . . I had been told that some whites in the audience would be in sympathy with me, some others would be there only out of curiosity, and many would be there to hear me make a fool of myself.

A Background Note about the Book

Published in 1901, *Up from Slavery* is the autobiography of Booker T. Washington (1856–1915), who was born a slave. The book also tells the story of major American events in the second half of the 1800s.

By reading Booker T. Washington's experiences as a young slave, we too experience slavery's final years. Washington describes his owner's Virginia plantation during the Civil War (1861–1865), giving us a slave's view of the conflict. Through his narrative, we are present when all slaves are freed at the war's end.

Following the war comes the Reconstruction period (1865–1877). We see Washington and other ex-slaves struggle for an education, adequate wages, and respectful treatment.

Finally, Washington takes us into the South's industrial age at the close of the 1800s. With experience ranging from coal mining to farming, he teaches other blacks how to use the most efficient tools, machines, and methods to produce crops, manufacture goods, and manage businesses. He is, in fact, a leader of the South's industrial revolution.

Booker T. Washington

UP
FROM
SLAVERY:

An Autobiography

Edited, and with an Afterword,
by Joan Dunayer

 THE TOWNSEND LIBRARY

UP FROM SLAVERY:
AN AUTOBIOGRAPHY

TP **THE TOWNSEND LIBRARY**

For more titles in the Townsend Library,
visit our website: **www.townsendpress.com**

All new material in this edition is
copyright © 2004 by Townsend Press.
Printed in the United States of America

0 9 8 7 6 5

ISBN-13: 978-1-59194-031-9
ISBN-10: 1-59194-031-1

Library of Congress Control Number:
2004105874

TABLE OF CONTENTS

AFTERWORD

CHAPTER 1

A SLAVE AMONG SLAVES

I was born a slave on a plantation, owned by James Burroughs, in Franklin County, Virginia. I do not know the exact place or date of my birth, but the time was spring 1856.

My earliest memories are of the plantation and its slave quarters, where the slaves had their cabins. Compared to other slave owners, the Burroughses were not especially cruel, but my life began in miserable surroundings. I was born in a typical log cabin about sixteen feet long and fourteen feet wide. I lived there with my mother, Jane; my brother, John, who is several years older than I am; and my half-sister, Amanda.

I know almost nothing about my ancestry. In the days of slavery, blacks' family histories received little attention. The purchase of a slave was noted in the same way as the purchase of a horse or cow.

In the slave quarters I heard whispered conversations about the tortures that slaves suffered on the ships that brought them from Africa to America. At least one of my maternal ancestors was among those slaves. As for my father—I don't even know his name. I have heard that he was a white man who lived on a nearby plantation. Whoever he was, he apparently never took the least interest in me or provided in any way for my upbringing.

The one-room cabin in which my family lived was not only our home but also the plantation's kitchen. My mother was the plantation's cook. The cabin had no glass windows, only side openings that let in light as well as winter's cold air. The cabin's door had large cracks, hung poorly on its hinges, and was too small for its opening.

In the cabin's lower right corner was a cat hole, something that almost every pre-Civil War mansion or cabin in Virginia possessed. The cat hole was a square opening, about seven by eight inches, that allowed cats to go in and out during the night. I never could understand why *our* cabin needed a cat hole: at least a half-dozen other openings in the cabin would have accommodated the cats.

Our cabin's floor was bare earth. In the

center of the floor was a large, deep opening covered with boards. During the winter, we stored sweet potatoes in this hole. While putting potatoes into this hole, or taking them out, I often would come into possession of one or two, which I roasted and thoroughly enjoyed.

Our plantation had no stove. My mother had to do all the cooking for the whites and slaves at the fireplace, mostly in pots and pans. Just as the cabin's poor construction caused us to suffer from cold in the winter, the fireplace caused us to suffer from heat in the summer.

My life's early years, which were spent in the little cabin, were not very different from those of thousands of other slaves. During the day, my mother could devote little time to her children. She would snatch a few moments for our care in the early morning before her work began and at night after her work was done.

One of my earliest memories is of my mother cooking a chicken late at night and awakening John, Amanda, and me so that we could eat it. I don't know how or where she got the chicken. I assume it came from the Burroughses' farm.

I can't remember a single time during my childhood that my entire family sat down to a table together and ate a meal in a civilized way. On the plantation the children got their meals very much as animals get theirs. We got a piece of bread here and a scrap of meat there, a cup of milk at one time and some potatoes at another. Sometimes members of our family would eat from the pot or frying pan while someone else ate from a tin plate held on their knees. Often we held our food with nothing but our hands.

Once a week I got to eat molasses. Our usual diet was cornbread and pork, but on Sunday morning my mother was permitted to bring down a little molasses from the "big house" (as the master's house was called) for John, Amanda, and me. I would get my tin plate and hold it up for the sweet morsel—about two tablespoons. I always shut my eyes while the molasses was being poured into the plate, in the hope that when I opened them, I'd be surprised to see how much I had gotten. When I opened my eyes, I'd tip the plate in one direction after another, to make the molasses spread all over it. I believed that there would be more molasses and it would last longer if it was spread out.

Once, I saw two of my young mistresses and some lady visitors eating ginger cakes in the yard. I felt that, if I ever was free, I would reach the height of my ambition if I obtained and ate ginger cakes.

My first pair of shoes had rough leather on top; the soles, about an inch thick, were wooden. When I walked, the shoes made considerable noise. They were uncomfortable because they didn't conform to the foot's shape or pressure.

However, wearing a flaxen shirt was a worse ordeal. In the part of Virginia where I lived, flax commonly was used in slave clothing—the cheapest and roughest flax. Putting on a new flaxen shirt was almost like having dozens of chestnut burrs against my skin, which was soft and tender. Several times that I was given a new flaxen shirt, John generously wore it for several days, to break it in, before I started to wear it. Until I was quite a youth, a flaxen shirt was the only garment that I wore.

John, Amanda, and I had no bed. We slept in and on a bundle of filthy rags laid on the dirt floor.

Nor did we have any playtime. Most of my time was spent cleaning the yards, carrying water to the men in the fields, or (once a week) bringing corn to the mill, for grinding.

I always dreaded bringing corn to the mill, which was about three miles from the plantation. The heavy bag of corn would be thrown across a horse's back, with about half of the corn on the horse's right and about half on the left. On almost every trip the corn would shift so that it became unbalanced. It would fall off the horse, and often I'd fall with it. Because I wasn't strong enough to reload the corn onto the horse, I'd have to wait, sometimes for hours, until some passerby came along who would help me. I usually spent the hours of waiting crying. The wait made me late in reaching the mill. By the time I got the corn ground and returned home, it was far into the night. The road was lonely and often led through dense forests. I always was frightened. The woods were said to be full of deserters from the Confederate army. I was told that a deserter would cut off the ears of any black boy whom he found alone. Whenever I got home late, I was scolded or flogged.

I had no schooling. Several times I carried the books of one of my young mistresses as far as the schoolhouse door. Seeing several dozen boys and girls engaged in study made a deep impression on me. I felt that getting into a schoolhouse and studying in this way must be like getting into Heaven.

I learned that I was a slave, and that

emancipation was being discussed, one morning before dawn. I was awakened by my mother kneeling over John, Amanda, and me and fervently praying that Abraham Lincoln and his armies would succeed and that she and her children would be freed.

From the time that William Lloyd Garrison, Elijah Lovejoy, and others began to agitate for freedom, slaves throughout the South kept in close touch with the progress of the anti-slavery movement. My mother and other slaves on the Burroughs plantation had many whispered late-night discussions. They understood the situation and kept themselves informed of events through the "grapevine."

When Lincoln was first campaigning to be President, the slaves on our plantation—miles from any railroad, large city, or daily newspaper—knew what issues were involved. When the Civil War began, even the most ignorant slaves on remote plantations felt certain that if the Northern armies prevailed, slavery would end.

Every Union victory and every Confederate defeat was a subject of intense interest. On our plantation this news usually came from the slave who was sent to the post office, about three miles away, for the mail, which came once or twice a week. After getting their mail, whites would congregate at the post office to discuss the latest news. The slave who was sent to the post office would linger long enough to get the drift of their conversation. On his way back, he would share the news with other slaves. In this way slaves often heard of important events before their owners did.

When I became big enough, I was required to go to the "big house" at mealtimes, to fan the flies from the table by means of a large set of pulley-operated paper fans. Much of the white people's conversation focused on the war and the end of slavery, and I absorbed much of it.

As the war continued, whites often found it difficult to get the food that they wanted. The usual slave diet of cornbread and pork could be obtained on the plantation, but coffee, tea, sugar, and other items to which the whites were accustomed frequently could not. The whites often used parched corn in place of coffee, and black molasses in place of sugar. Often they didn't use anything to sweeten their tea and so-called coffee.

During the war one of my young masters was killed, and two were severely wounded. The slaves on our plantation felt genuine sorrow when they heard that "Mas'er Billy" was dead. Some of the slaves had nursed him; others had played with him when he was a child; still others had known him to beg for mercy when they were being thrashed by James Burroughs or the overseer. When the two young masters were brought home wounded, some slaves begged to sit up at night to nurse them.

While the white males were off fighting in the war, many slaves would have died to protect the white women and children on the plantations. The slave who was selected to sleep in the "big house" during the absence of the white males was considered to have the place of honor. Anyone attempting to harm "young Mistress" or "old Mistress" during the night would have had to cross the slave's dead body to do so.

I know of blacks who have tenderly cared for former masters and mistresses who became dependent after the war; blacks who have given their former owners money, to keep them from suffering; and blacks who have assisted in the education of their former owners' descendants. On one large Southern plantation, a young white man, the son of the estate's former owner, has become poor and a drunkard. Notwithstanding their own poverty, the blacks on this plantation have, for years, supplied him with life's necessities. One sends him a little coffee or sugar, another a little meat, and so on.

The whole machinery of slavery discouraged white self-reliance. It made labor a badge of degradation and inferiority. To my knowledge, not one of James Burroughs's many children ever mastered a single trade or craft. In general, slave owners and their children learned no skills or trades. From cooking and sewing to carpentry and farming, manual labor was left to slaves. When freedom came, many former slaves were almost as well prepared to begin life anew as their former masters, except with regard to literacy and ownership of property.

Fearful of "Yankee" invasions, whites had their silverware and other valuables taken from the "big house," buried in the woods, and guarded by trusted slaves. The slaves would give Yankee soldiers food, drink, clothing, anything except something specifically entrusted to their care.

Not long ago in a small Ohio town, I met a former slave from Virginia who exemplified many slaves' sense of honor. Two or three years before the Emancipation Proclamation, this man and his master made a contract to the effect that he would be permitted to buy himself by paying a certain amount each year. Meanwhile, he would be permitted to labor where and for whom he chose. Finding that he could get better wages in Ohio, he went there. When freedom came, he still owed his former master about $300, according to their contract. Although the Emancipation Proclamation had freed him from any obligation to his former master, this man walked most of the way back to where his former master lived in Virginia and placed the last dollar, with interest, in his hands. The man told me that he knew that he needn't pay the debt but that he never broke his word.

For months, freedom's approach was in the air. Every day, we saw army deserters returning to their homes. Others who had been discharged, or whose regiments had been paroled, continually passed by. News of great events swiftly traveled from one plantation to another.

As freedom neared, the singing in the slave quarters became bolder, had more ring, and lasted later into the night. Most verses of the plantation songs contained some reference to freedom. The slaves had sung those same verses before but had been careful to say that "freedom" referred to the next world. Now they let it be known that the "freedom" in their songs meant freedom in *this* world.

Finally the war ended. One night in 1865, word was sent to the slave quarters that something unusual was going to take place at the "big house" the next morning. There was little, if any, sleep that night. All was excitement and expectation.

Early the next morning all the slaves gathered at the house. All members of the Burroughs family were standing or sitting on the veranda. Their faces had a look of deep interest, perhaps sadness.

A stranger (probably a U.S. officer) made a short speech and then read a rather long paper: the Emancipation Proclamation, I think. After the reading we all were told that we were free. We could go when and where we pleased. I was nine years old.

My mother, who was standing by my side, leaned over and kissed John, Amanda, and me. Tears of joy ran down her cheeks. She explained to us what it all meant. She said that this was the day for which she had prayed—the day that she had feared she never would live to see.

For some minutes there was great rejoicing and thanksgiving. But by the time the blacks returned to their cabins, they were more subdued. The great responsibility of being free, of having to think and plan for themselves and their children, took hold of them. They were like youths of ten or twelve turned out into the world to provide for themselves. Is it any wonder that within a few hours, gloom seemed to pervade the slave quarters?

Some of the slaves were seventy or eighty years old; their best days were gone. They had no strength with which to earn a living in a strange place and among strangers, even if they had known where to find a new home. Also, they felt an attachment to "old Mas'er," "old Missus," and their children that they found hard to break. In some cases, they had spent nearly half a century with the Burroughses. One by one, stealthily at first, the older slaves began to wander from the slave quarters back to the "big house" to have a whispered conversation with the Burroughses as to the future.

CHAPTER 2

BOYHOOD DAYS

Slaves had only a first name or a first name combined with their owner's last name. For example, a slave who belonged to a white man named Hatcher might be Jane Hatcher, Hatcher's Jane, or simply Jane. After emancipation, most blacks took new last names, such as Lincoln or Johnson. Many also used a middle initial that didn't stand for any name but was part of what blacks proudly called their "entitles."

Most blacks left their plantation for at least a few days or weeks, to see what freedom was like. After a while, many elderly slaves returned to their old homes and made some kind of contract with their former owners, by which they remained on the estate.

My mother's husband, Washington Ferguson, who was Amanda's father and the stepfather of John and me, had belonged to a different owner than my mother. In fact, he seldom had come to the Burroughs plantation. I had seen him there perhaps once a year, around Christmas time. During the war he had run away. Apparently by following Union soldiers, he had found his way to the new state of West Virginia. As soon as freedom was declared, he sent for my mother to come to West Virginia's Kanawha Valley.

Neither my mother nor any of her children ever had been far from the Burroughs plantation. At that time a journey from Virginia over the mountains to West Virginia was quite an undertaking. We placed what little clothing and few household goods we had in a cart and walked most of the distance, which was several hundred miles. Most of the time we slept in the open air and did our cooking outdoors, over a log fire. One night we camped near an abandoned log cabin. My mother decided to build a cooking fire inside the cabin and, afterward, make up some kind of bedding on the floor. Just as the fire got well started, a black snake a yard and a half long dropped down the chimney and hurried out onto the floor. We immediately abandoned the cabin.

The trip took us several weeks. Our destination was a small town called Malden, about five miles from Charleston, West Virginia's present capital.

My stepfather had obtained a little cabin for us to live in. Our new house was no better than the one we had left on the Burroughs plantation. In one respect it was worse. In our plantation cabin, we always had been assured of fresh air, but our new home was in a cluster of cabins crowded together. Because there were no sanitary regulations, the filth around the cabins often was intolerable. Some of our neighbors were blacks; some were the poorest, most ignorant, and most degraded whites. Drinking, gambling, fighting, and loose sex were common.

At that time, salt mining was the main industry in Malden's part of West Virginia. Everyone in Malden was connected with the salt business. My stepfather already had a job at a salt furnace. Although I was only a child, he put John and me to work in one of the furnaces. Often I began work as early as 4 a.m.

I acquired my first reading ability while working in this salt furnace. The barrels of each salt packer were marked with a particular number. My stepfather's number was 18. At the end of a day's work, the packers' boss would come around and put "18" on each of our barrels. I soon learned to recognize that number wherever I saw it; after a while I could write it.

From the time that I can remember having any thoughts about anything, I had felt an intense desire to learn to read. When I was a small child, I decided that, if I accomplished nothing else in life, I somehow would get enough education to be able to read common books and newspapers.

Soon after my family settled into our Malden cabin, I persuaded my mother to get me a book. Somehow she obtained an old copy of a spelling book that contained the alphabet, followed by letter combinations such as *ab*, *ba*, *ca*, and *da*. I immediately began to devour this book, the first one that I think I ever had in my hands.

Someone had told me that the way to begin to read was to learn the alphabet. I had no one to teach me. At that time there wasn't a black anywhere near us who could read, and I was too timid to approach a white. Somehow, within a few weeks, I mastered most of the alphabet. In all my efforts to learn to read, my mother encouraged me and aided me in every way that she could. Although she was illiterate, she had high ambitions for her children.

In the midst of my struggles and longing for an education, a young black man who had learned to read in Ohio came to Malden. As soon as the blacks found out that he could read, they got a newspaper. At the end of nearly every day's work, this man was surrounded by men and women anxious to hear him read the news in the papers. How I envied him! To me, he was a man who must be completely satisfied with his achievements.

About this time Malden's blacks began to discuss having some kind of school for the children. It would be the first school for black children in the Kanawha Valley—a great event—so the discussion excited wide interest.

The most perplexing question was where to find a teacher. The young man from Ohio was considered, but he seemed too young. Soon another young black man from Ohio arrived in Malden. He had been a soldier and possessed considerable education. The black people hired him to teach at their first school.

At that time, there weren't any free schools for blacks in the Kanawha Valley, so each family agreed to pay a certain amount per month, with the understanding that the teacher would "board around" (spend one day with each family). This arrangement wasn't bad for the teacher because each family tried to provide the very best on the day that he was their guest. I looked forward to "teacher's day" at our little cabin.

Blacks were eager for an education. Few were too young or old to attempt to learn. As fast as teachers could be obtained, day schools and night schools were filled. The great ambition of the older blacks was to learn to read the Bible before they died. With this end in view, many blacks who were fifty or older attended night school. Sunday schools were formed soon after freedom, but the spelling book was the principal book studied there. Day school, night school, and Sunday school always were crowded. Often, many people had to be turned away due to lack of room.

However, the opening of the Kanawha Valley school brought one of the sharpest disappointments of my life. I had been working in a salt furnace for several months, and my stepfather had discovered that I had financial value. So, when the school opened, he decided that he couldn't spare me from my work. From my workplace, I could see happy children going to and from school, mornings and afternoons. I worked harder than ever at mastering the contents of my spelling book.

After a while, my mother arranged for the school teacher to give me lessons at night, after my day's work. I greatly welcomed these night lessons. Still, my heart was set on going to the day school. Finally I was permitted to go to the day school for a few months, provided that I rose early in the morning, worked in the furnace until 9 a.m., and returned there immediately after school for at least two more hours of work.

The schoolhouse was some distance from the furnace. I had to work until 9 a.m., and the school day began at the same hour. To get around this difficulty, I yielded to temptation. There was a large clock in a little office in the furnace. All of the workers—a hundred or more—depended on this clock to determine when they began and ended their day's work. To enable me to reach school on time, I moved the clock's hands from 8:30 to 9:00. I did this morning after morning, until the furnace boss realized that something was wrong and locked the clock inside a case.

When I went to the school for the first time, I found that all of the other children had caps. I never had worn any head covering or even thought about wearing one. But when I saw how all the other boys were dressed, I felt uncomfortable. As usual, I put the case before my mother. She said that she had no money with which to buy a "store hat" (at that time, a novelty among blacks that was considered quite the thing for young and old), but that she would find a solution. She got two pieces of denim and sewed them together, and I became the proud possessor of my first cap. Several of my schoolmates who had store-bought caps made fun of my homemade one, but I never have been as proud of any other hat or cap.

My name presented another problem. I always had been called simply "Booker." Before going to school, I never had encountered any need for a last name. But when I heard the school roll called, I noticed that all of the other children had both a first and a last name. Some of them—extravagantly—had a middle name as well. What should I do? By the time the teacher asked my name, I calmly answered, "Booker Washington," as if I had been called that all my life. Later in life, I would discover that my mother had given me the name Booker Taliaferro soon after I was born. I then adopted the name Booker Taliaferro Washington.

More than once I have tried to picture myself in the position of someone with a distinguished ancestry that he can trace back hundreds of years—someone who has inherited not only a name but a fortune and a proud family homestead. Yet, if I had inherited these and been white, maybe I would have depended on my ancestry and skin color to do for me what I should do for myself. Because I had no such privileges, I resolved years ago that I would leave a record that my children would be proud of and that would encourage them to still-greater effort.

The period during which I was permitted to attend day school was short, and my attendance was irregular. Soon I had to devote all of my time to work.

I again resorted to night schooling. In fact, most of my boyhood education was obtained through night schooling. I often had difficulty finding a satisfactory teacher. Sometimes, after I had found someone to teach me, I would discover that the teacher knew little more than I did. Often I had to walk several miles at night to have lessons. Throughout my youth, no matter how discouraging my circumstances were, I remained determined to obtain an education.

Although my family was poor, my mother adopted an orphan boy soon after we moved to Malden. We named him James B. Washington. He has been a member of the family ever since.

After I had worked in the salt furnace for some time, work was secured for me in a coal mine. I intensely disliked working in the mine. I always was unclean while at work and found it hard to get my skin clean when the day's work was done. Also, the distance from the mine's entrance to the coal was a full mile of blackest darkness. The mine was divided into many rooms. Because I never was able to learn the location of all these rooms, I got lost in the mine many times. Adding to the horror of being lost, my light sometimes went out. If I didn't happen to have a match, I would wander around in the darkness until I found someone to give me a light.

The work was dangerous and hard. There always was the chance of being blown to pieces by a premature powder explosion or of being crushed by falling slate. Such accidents occurred frequently and kept me in constant fear.

Many young children were forced to work in coal mines. They had little opportunity to get an education and often were physically and mentally stunted. Most soon lost the ambition to do anything other than continue as a coal miner.

CHAPTER 3

THE STRUGGLE FOR
FOR AN EDUCATION

One day in the coal mine, I overheard two miners talking about a Virginia school called the Hampton Normal and Agricultural Institute. In the mine's darkness, I noiselessly crept as close as I could to the two men. One told the other that the school had been established for blacks and that poor students could work for their board while learning a trade or profession. As the man continued describing Hampton, I resolved to go there someday.

A few months later, I heard about a vacant position in the household of General Lewis Ruffner, the mine's owner. His wife, Viola Ruffner, was a "Yankee" from Vermont. She had a reputation of being very strict with her servants, especially the boys. Few of them remained with her more than two or three weeks. I decided that I would rather try the

Ruffner house than remain in the coal mine, so my mother applied to Mrs. Ruffner about the vacant position. I was hired at a salary of $5 per month.

Mrs. Ruffner wanted everything kept clean, neat, and in good repair. She wanted things done promptly and carefully. And she wanted absolute honesty. I soon went from fearing her to considering her one of my best friends. When she found that she could trust me, she did so completely. During the winter months, she allowed me to go to school for an hour each day. But I did most of my studying at night—sometimes alone, sometimes with someone I hired to teach me. I made a book-case out of a wooden box and began putting into it every book that I could get my hands on. I called the collection my "library."

I lived with Mrs. Ruffner about a year and a half. The lessons that I learned in her home were as valuable to me as any education that I have received since. To this day I never see bits of paper scattered around a house or in the street without wanting to pick them up. I never see a filthy yard that I do not want to clean, an unpainted house that I do not want to paint, or a missing button on a piece of clothing that I do not want to replace.

In fall 1872, when I was sixteen, I decided to go to Hampton. My family had used all of my earnings except for a few dollars, so I had very little money with which to buy clothes and pay traveling expenses. John helped me all that he could, but that wasn't much because he worked in the coal mine, where he earned little, and most of his earnings went toward paying the household expenses. I was touched by the interest that many older blacks showed in my going to Hampton. They had spent the best days of their lives in slavery and hardly had expected to see a black child attend a boarding school. Some of these older people gave me a nickel or a quarter.

Finally the day of my departure arrived. I started for Hampton with only a small, cheap satchel containing a few articles of clothing.

At that time there were no trains connecting the Malden area with eastern Virginia. Trains went only part of the way; the rest of the distance had to be traveled by stagecoach.

After traveling over the mountains most of the afternoon, the stagecoach in which I was a passenger stopped, late at night, at an unpainted house that was a hotel. All of my fellow passengers were white. After they had been shown rooms and were getting ready for supper, I shyly presented myself before the man at the desk. I had practically no money. I was hoping to beg my way into the landlord's good graces and obtain some food and lodging, especially because it was cold outside. Without asking whether I had any money, the man at the desk firmly refused to consider giving me food or lodging. This was my first experience as to what my skin color still meant after emancipation. I spent that night outside, trying to keep warm by walking around.

The distance from Malden to Hampton is about five hundred miles. I hadn't been away from home many hours before it became painfully evident that I didn't have enough money to pay stagecoach fare all the way to Hampton.

By walking, and by begging rides in wagons and carts, after some days I reached Richmond, Virginia, about eighty-two miles from Hampton. It was late at night. I was tired, hungry, dirty, and completely out of money. I never had been in a large city before. I knew no one in Richmond and did not know where to go. I asked for lodging at several places, but they all wanted money. Not knowing what else to do, I walked the streets. I passed by many food stands where pieces of fried chicken and half-moon apple pies were piled high. I would have promised all that I expected to possess in the future for one chicken leg or pie.

Some time after midnight, I came across a raised portion of board sidewalk. I waited a few minutes, until I was sure that no passers-by could see me. Then I crept under the boardwalk and lay on the ground, with my satchel as a pillow. Nearly all night I could hear the tramp of feet over my head.

The next morning I found myself somewhat refreshed but extremely hungry. As soon as it was light enough for me to see my surroundings, I saw that I was near a large ship that was unloading a cargo of pig iron. I went to the ship and asked the captain, a white man, if I could help unload the iron for some money. He consented. I worked long enough to earn money for my breakfast, which seemed the best breakfast I ever had eaten.

The captain was so pleased with my work that he said I could continue to work for a small amount of pay each day. I worked on the ship for some days, sleeping under the boardwalk each night.

When I had saved enough money to reach Hampton, I thanked the captain for his kindness and resumed travel. I reached Hampton with exactly fifty cents.

My first sight of the three-story brick school rewarded me for all that I had suffered in order to reach the place. It seemed the largest, most beautiful building that I ever had seen.

I presented myself before the head

teacher, Mary Mackie, for assignment to a class. Having been so long without proper food, a bath, and a change of clothing, I did not make a favorable impression on her. For several hours I lingered around her, trying to impress her with my worthiness, as she admitted other students but neither accepted nor rejected *me*. Then she said to me, "The adjoining recitation room needs sweeping. Take the broom and sweep it."

I swept the recitation room three times. Then I got a dusting cloth and dusted it four times—every desk, table, and bench, and all the woodwork around the walls. I also moved every piece of furniture and thoroughly cleaned every closet and corner in the room.

Then I reported to Miss Mackie. She went into the room and inspected the floor and closets. She took her handkerchief and rubbed it over the table, the benches, and the woodwork around the walls. When she was unable to find any dirt or dust, she said, "I guess you will do to enter this institution." The sweeping of that room was my examination, and no young man ever passed an exam for entrance into Harvard or Yale with greater joy or satisfaction than I passed that exam.

Miss Mackie offered me a position as janitor. I gladly accepted. The job would pay for most of my board. I had to care for many rooms and work late into the night. In addition, I had to rise by 4 a.m. to build the fires and have some time to prepare my lessons.

Life at Hampton was a constant revelation. Using a toothbrush; bathing in a tub; eating meals at regular hours, with a tablecloth and a napkin—all these things were new to me.

For some time at Hampton, I owned only one pair of socks. I would wear these until they became soiled, then wash them at night and hang them by the fire to dry, so that I could wear them again the next morning.

The charge for my board at Hampton was $10 a month. I was expected to pay part of this in cash and work out the rest. But aside from a few dollars that John was able to send me once in a while, I had no money. I made my janitorial work so indispensable that I soon was told that it would cover the full cost of my board.

Tuition was $70 a year, far beyond my means. Hampton's principal, General Samuel C. Armstrong, who had been in the Union army, arranged for me to receive a full scholarship.

Because I couldn't afford books, I borrowed them from other students. Clothes were another problem. General Armstrong personally inspected the young men, in ranks, to see that their clothes were clean. Shoes had to be polished. No grease spots or missing buttons were permitted. To wear one suit of clothes continually, at work and in the school-room, and keep it clean was difficult. Some of the teachers gave me secondhand clothing from barrels sent from the North. These barrels were a blessing to hundreds of poor students.

At Hampton I initially shared a room with seven other boys because space was at a premium. My bed had two sheets, something new in my experience. Puzzled, I slept under both sheets the first night. The second night I slept *on top of* both. Finally, by watching the other boys, I realized that I was expected to sleep *between* the two sheets.

I was one of the youngest students. Most were adults, some as old as forty. Hampton's several hundred students were tremendously earnest. They spent every hour studying or working. Yet some of the students were unable to master the textbooks; it made me sad to watch their struggles. Besides having to wrestle with their books, many of the students were so poor that they had to struggle for life's necessities. Many had elderly parents who were dependent on them; some were married men who had to support their wives.

CHAPTER

4

HELPING OTHERS

At the end of my first year at Hampton, most of the students and teachers went home for vacation. I was homesick but had no money for travel. I decided to sell a second-hand coat that I had received. I told a few people in the town of Hampton that I had a coat to sell, and, after much persuading, one black man came to my room to see the coat. After looking the garment over, he asked me how much I wanted for it. I told him that I thought it was worth $3. He said, "I'll take the coat. I'll pay you five cents now and the rest as soon as I can get it." With that "offer," I gave up all hope of visiting my family.

I decided to go where I could earn money for much-needed clothing and other necessities. After several days of trying to find work in or near the town of Hampton, I finally got work in a restaurant at Fortress Monroe. The wages were scarcely more than my board. At night and between meals, I found time for reading and study.

I owed Hampton Institute $16 that I hadn't been able to work out. I had hoped to earn enough money over the summer to pay off this debt, but when the end of vacation approached, I didn't have the $16.

During my last week at the restaurant, I found a $10 bill under one of the tables. I felt obligated to show the money to the restaurant's owner. When I did, he said that because the restaurant was his place of business, he had a right to keep the money. He shared none of it with me.

When my restaurant job ended, I went to Hampton's treasurer, General J.F.B. Marshall, and explained my situation. Much to my relief, he said that I could return to Hampton and pay the debt when I was able. During my second year at Hampton, I continued to work as a janitor.

One of the things that impressed me the most about Hampton was the unselfishness of its teachers, who were white "Yankees." They were devoted to the students. I learned that the happiest people are those who do the most for others.

Nathalie Lord, a teacher from Maine, taught me to appreciate the Bible not only for the spiritual help that it offers but also as literature. She also taught me much about public speaking. When she discovered that I had some inclination in that direction, she gave me private lessons on breathing, emphasis, and articulation.

Hampton's debating society was a constant source of delight to me. It held debates every Saturday evening. I think that I didn't miss a single one.

Between the time that supper ended and evening study began, there was about twenty minutes that the young men usually spent in idle gossip. About twenty of us students organized another debating society, to make better use of this time.

At the end of my second year at Hampton, I was able to return to Malden for summer vacation because John and my mother sent me money and one of my teachers supplemented that amount with a small gift. My family was overjoyed to see me.

The joy of all classes of black people, especially the older ones, over my return was almost pathetic. I had to take a meal with each family and tell of my experiences at Hampton I also had to address the church, the Sunday school, and various other groups.

I spent most of the first month of my vacation trying to find work. Neither the salt furnaces nor the coal mine was operating because the miners were on strike.

Toward the end of the month, I went to a place a considerable distance from my home, seeking employment. I didn't succeed. It was night before I started back. When I was within a mile or so of my home, I was too tired to walk any farther, so I went into an old, abandoned house to spend the rest of the night. About 3 a.m. John found me asleep in this house. As gently as he could, he told me that our mother had died during the night.

This was the saddest moment of my life. For several years my mother had been in poor health, but when I had parted from her the previous day, she hadn't seemed near death. I always had wanted to be with her when she died. One of my chief motivations at Hampton had been my hope of someday being in a position to make her comfortable and happy. She often had expressed a wish to see her children educated and out in the world.

After my mother's death, my family's home was in confusion. Amanda did her best, but she was too young to know much about homemaking, and my stepfather was unable to hire a cook or housekeeper. More than once, a can of tomatoes and some crackers constituted a meal. The family's clothing went untended. Soon everything around the house was in tumble-down condition.

During this trying period, Mrs. Ruffner made me welcome at her home and assisted me in many ways. Before the end of my vacation, she gave me some work. This work, together with work in a coal mine some distance from my home, enabled me to earn enough money to travel back to Hampton.

Three weeks before Hampton's school year was to begin, I received a letter from Miss Mackie. She asked me to return two weeks early, to assist her in cleaning the buildings and getting things ready for the school year. This was just the opportunity that I wanted. It gave me a chance to secure a credit in the treasurer's office. I started for Hampton at once.

Although she belonged to a very cultured family, for two weeks Miss Mackie worked by my side cleaning windows, dusting rooms, putting beds in order, and doing other menial work. She did such work every year that I was at Hampton. At the time, it was hard for me to understand how a woman of her education and social standing could delight in such labor. I now understand that she felt no indignity in doing menial tasks, especially for others' benefit.

Hampton's dormitories became so crowded that it was impossible to find room for everyone who wanted to be admitted. General Armstrong asked if some of the older students would be willing to live in tents during the winter. Nearly every student volunteered, including me. The winter that some of us spent in those tents was intensely cold. We suffered but made no complaints. We were happy to make it possible for more students to get an education. More than once, when a stiff gale blew during a cold night, my tent was lifted bodily, and I found myself in the open air.

During my last year at Hampton, I spent nearly every minute either in janitorial work or intense study. I made the honor roll and in June 1875, at age nineteen, finished Hampton's regular course of study.

When I graduated, I was completely out of money. Some other Hampton students and I got waiter jobs at a summer hotel in Connecticut. I borrowed enough money to get there.

Although I had worked as a waiter, I knew

almost nothing about waiting on hotel tables. When the head waiter assigned me to a table with wealthy, aristocratic customers, they scolded me harshly for my awkwardness. I was so flustered that I left the table—left the customers sitting there without food. As a result, I was demoted from waiter to dish carrier. However, within a few weeks, I learned what was expected of a waiter and regained my former position. (I have had the satisfaction of being a guest in this hotel several times since I was a waiter there.)

When the hotel season ended, I returned to Malden and taught in the town's black school. I began work at 8 a.m., and it usually continued until 10 p.m. In addition to teaching standard academic content, I taught the pupils how to comb their hair, use a toothbrush, and keep their clothing, hands, and faces clean.

So many of Malden's adults and older children had to work during the day, but craved education, that I soon opened a night school. From the beginning, the night school was crowded, about as well attended as the school that I taught during the day.

I also established a small reading room and a debating society. On Sundays I taught two Sunday schools, one in the morning at a place three miles from Malden, the other in the afternoon in Malden.

In addition, I gave private lessons to several young men whom I was preparing for Hampton. Without regard to pay, I taught anyone who wanted to learn anything that I could teach. I received a small salary from the public fund for my work as a public-school teacher.

During my time at Hampton, John had assisted me all that he could while working in the coal mine to support our family. He had neglected his own education in order to advance mine. It was now my earnest wish to help him enter Hampton and to save money toward his expenses there. We succeeded. John finished Hampton's course of study in three years. When he returned from Hampton, we combined our efforts and savings to send our adopted brother, James, to Hampton. He, too, graduated.

I spent 1877, my second year teaching in Malden, much as I had spent the year before. At this time the Ku Klux Klan was at the height of its activity. The Klan consisted of bands of white men who had joined together to keep blacks from gaining influence and power. They resembled the "patrollers" of the time of slavery. The patrollers had been bands of white men—mostly young—who policed slaves at night, preventing them from going from one plantation to another without passes, preventing them from holding any meetings without permission and without the presence of at least one white man, and so on. Like the patrollers, Klansmen operated mostly at night. Their main objective was to crush blacks' political aspirations, but they also burned schoolhouses and churches and committed acts of violence against blacks, including murder.

As a young man, I was greatly affected by the Klan's actions. In Malden a battle took place between whites and blacks, with about a hundred people on each side. Many people on both sides were seriously injured. Trying to defend the blacks, General Ruffner was knocked down and was wounded so severely that he never fully recovered.

CHAPTER 5

RECONSTRUCTION
AND BEYOND

The years from 1865 to 1877 are called the Reconstruction period. Throughout the South during this period, both day and night schools overflowed with blacks of all conditions and ages, including people of sixty or seventy.

Most blacks who received a bit of education became teachers or preachers. Although many of these people were capable and earnest, many others took up teaching or preaching as an easy way to make a living. Many who could do little more than write their names became teachers.

I remember one black man who came into our neighborhood in search of a teaching job. He was asked how he would teach the children about the shape of the Earth. He said that he would teach either that the Earth was round or that it was flat, according to the preference of most of his patrons.

Many immoral men claimed that they were "called to preach," usually within a few days of learning to read. In Malden the "call" usually came when a man was sitting in church. Suddenly he would fall to the floor, as if struck by a bullet. He would lie there for hours, speechless and motionless. Then the news would spread throughout the neighborhood that this man had received a "call." In my youth I feared that when I learned to read and write well, I too would be "called."

Throughout Reconstruction, Southern blacks looked to the federal government for assistance. This was only natural. The federal government had given us freedom, and the whole nation had been enriched, for more than two centuries, by the labor of blacks. Even as a youth, I felt that it was cruelly wrong of the federal and state governments not to make some provision for the education of freed blacks.

In fall 1878, having taught school in Malden for two years and having succeeded in preparing my brothers and several other students to enter Hampton, I decided to spend some months studying at the Wayland

Seminary in Washington, D.C. At Wayland, students received no vocational training. In contrast, Hampton emphasized vocational education. Wayland students tended to have more money than Hampton students and dress in stylish clothes. Hampton students paid for their board, books, clothing, and room either wholly or partly by work. Many Wayland students had their personal expenses paid for them. Hampton students constantly strove to help themselves. Wayland students seemed less self-reliant. They paid more attention to outward appearances. When they graduated, they knew more Latin and Greek, but they seemed to know less about making their way in life. Having lived for a number of years in comfortable surroundings, they were less inclined than Hampton students to go into the South's rural areas, where there was little comfort, and work to help other blacks. They were more inclined to become hotel waiters or railroad porters.

I remained in Washington eight months. During that time, the city was crowded with blacks, many of whom had recently come from the South. Some had been drawn to Washington because they felt that they could lead a life of relative ease there. Others had obtained minor government positions. Still others hoped to obtain government positions. A number of black men—some of them quite brilliant—were in the House of Representatives. One was in the Senate. In Washington, blacks felt protected by the law. Also, the city's schools for blacks were better than they were elsewhere.

While many of the city's blacks seemed substantial and worthy, many others seemed superficial. I saw young black men who were not earning more than $4 a week spend $2 or more for a buggy in which they rode up and down Pennsylvania Avenue on Sunday, in an effort to convince the world that they were worth thousands. I saw other young black men who received $75 or $100 a month from the government, yet were in debt at the end of every month. I saw black men, unemployed and in poverty, who had been congressmen only a few months before.

In Washington I saw black girls whose mothers were earning their living by laundering and taught them that skill. Later these girls entered public schools and remained there perhaps six or eight years. When they finished the public school course, they wanted more—expensive dresses, shoes, and hats. Their desires had increased more than their ability to satisfy those desires. Their six or eight years of book education had weaned them away from their mother's occupation. They had received education that cultivates the mind (for example, in languages and mathematics) but no vocational training.

During this period, many of the young black men who went to school or college did so with the expressed determination to prepare themselves to be lawyers or congressmen. Many of the women planned to become music teachers. I felt that more must be done to prepare their way.

CHAPTER 6

BLACKS AND INDIANS

In 1879, when I was twenty-three, I received a letter from General Armstrong inviting me to give Hampton's next commencement address. I was pleased and honored.

When I traveled back to Hampton, I went over much of the same ground—now covered entirely by railroad—that I had traversed nearly six years before, when I first sought admittance to Hampton. At Hampton I received a warm welcome from the teachers and students. During my absence, the institute's vocational and academic training had greatly improved.

Soon after I returned to Malden, I was surprised to receive another letter from General Armstrong. This one asked me to return to Hampton partly as a teacher and partly to pursue additional studies. My brothers and the four other students whom I had prepared for Hampton had arrived there so well-prepared that they had entered advanced classes. This fact, it seems, had led to my being offered a Hampton teaching position.

About this time, Hampton began to admit Indians as well as blacks. More than a hundred Indians, most of them young men, would be coming from reservations in the West. General Armstrong wished me to be a "house father" to the Indian young men—live in the building with them and take charge of their discipline, clothing, rooms, and so on. I had become so absorbed in my West Virginia teaching that I was sorry to give it up, but I didn't feel that I could refuse General Armstrong after all his assistance to me.

At Hampton I took up residence in a building with about seventy-five Indian youths. I was the only non-Indian in the building. To my relief, I soon earned the students' affection and respect.

The things that the Indian students most disliked, I think, were to have their long hair cut, to give up wearing their blankets, and to stop smoking. In my experience, most whites don't think that members of any other race are wholly civilized until they wear the same clothing, eat the same food, speak the same language, and profess the same religion as whites.

The Indian students faced the added difficulty of having to learn English. Whenever they were asked to do so, black students gladly took the Indians as roommates, in order to help them learn English and acquire "civilized" habits. Some of the black students felt that the Indians shouldn't have been admitted to Hampton, but they were in the minority.

This reminds me of a conversation that I once had with Frederick Douglass. Once, while traveling by train in Pennsylvania, Mr. Douglass was forced, because of his color, to ride in the baggage car, even though he had paid the same price for his ticket as the other passengers. Some white passengers went into the baggage car to apologize to him. "Mr. Douglass, I am sorry that you have been degraded in this manner," one of them said. Mr. Douglass straightened himself up on the box on which he was sitting and replied that *he* was not the one degraded by such treatment; the degraded ones were those who *inflicted* it.

In one part of our country, where the law demands segregation of blacks and whites on trains, I once witnessed a related incident. There was a man whose community knew him to be black, but whose appearance was white. He was riding in the part of the train set aside for black passengers. Upon reaching him, the conductor appeared perplexed. He looked the passenger over carefully, examining his hair, eyes, nose, and hands, but still seemed puzzled. Finally he stooped over and peeped at the man's feet. Whether or not that settled the matter, the conductor allowed the passenger to remain where he was.

While I was in charge of the Indian boys at Hampton, I had two experiences that illustrate the curious workings of racism in America. One of the Indian boys fell ill, and I needed to bring him to the Department of the Interior, in Washington, so that he could be returned to his reservation. During our journey on a steamboat, I was careful not to enter the dining room when the dinner bell rang. Instead I waited until most of the passengers had finished their meal. Then the Indian boy and I went to the dining room. The steward politely informed me that waiters could serve the Indian boy, but not me. The boy and I had nearly the same skin color, but somehow the steward knew exactly where to draw the color line. Hampton had directed me to stay at a particular hotel in Washington, but when the Indian boy and I went to this hotel, the clerk stated that he would be glad to provide lodging for the boy, but not for me.

Another incident demonstrated equal irrationality. I found myself in a town that was so agitated that a lynching seemed likely. The cause of all the outrage was the fact that a dark-skinned man had stopped at the local hotel. Investigation revealed that he was a visitor from Morocco who spoke English. As soon as it was learned that he was not an *American* black, all signs of indignation disappeared. Thereafter, however, the Moroccan decided it would be wise not to speak English while in this country.

At the end of my first year with the Indian students, another Hampton position opened for me. Numerous young blacks wished to receive an education but were too poor to attend Hampton, so General Armstrong decided to start a Hampton night school that would accept a limited number of the most promising of these young men and women, on condition that they work at the institute ten hours during the day and attend school for two hours at night. They would be paid more than the cost of their board for their work. Most of their earnings would be placed in the school's treasury as funds to be drawn on to pay their board when they became students in the day school, after one or two years of night school. General Armstrong asked me to take charge of the night school, and I did. Meanwhile, I continued my own studies under the direction of Hampton instructors.

Initially about a dozen young men and women entered the night school. During the day most of the men worked in the school's sawmill, and the women worked in the laundry. The night-school pupils were good students who mastered their work. Only the ringing of the night bell made them stop studying. Often they would urge me to continue the lessons beyond the customary bedtime.

The night-school students worked so hard, both at their day work and their evening studies, that I named them "The Plucky Class." When students proved themselves in the night school, I gave them a printed certificate that read something like this: "This is to certify that Jane Smith is a member of 'The Plucky Class' of the Hampton Institute and is in good standing." The students prized these certificates, which added to the night school's popularity.

Within a few weeks about twenty-five students were in attendance. I have followed the course of many of those twenty-five men and women since then. They now hold important, useful positions in nearly every part of the South.

CHAPTER 7

EARLY DAYS AT TUSKEGEE

In 1881, near the close of my first year teaching the night school, General Armstrong told me that he had received a letter from two Alabama men asking him to recommend someone to head a planned teachers' school, for blacks, in the Alabama town of Tuskegee. These men seemed to assume that no suitable black could be found; they were expecting General Armstrong to recommend a white. But he asked me if I thought that I could fill the position. I told him that I would try. Accordingly, he wrote back recommending me.

Several days later, during Sunday evening chapel service, a messenger came in and handed the general a telegram. At the end of the service, he read the telegram to the school. It said, "Booker T. Washington will suit us. Send him at once." The students and teachers expressed much joy and congratulations.

I immediately prepared to go. I went to Malden, where I stayed several days, and then proceeded to Tuskegee. I was twenty-five.

Tuskegee was a town of about two thousand residents, nearly half of whom were black. It was in the South's "black belt," in a county in which blacks outnumbered whites by about three to one. In some nearby counties, the ratio was about six blacks to one white.

Tuskegee was rather secluded, connected by a short railroad line to the railroad's main line, about five miles away. During slavery and since, the town had been a center of education, so its white residents tended to be exceptionally cultivated and educated. In general, the relations between blacks and whites were pleasant. For example, a black man and a white man jointly owned and operated the town's hardware store.

Before going to Tuskegee, I had expected to find there a building and all the necessary equipment for me to begin teaching. I found nothing of the kind. I *did* find hundreds of people eager to learn and many black citizens eager to help get the school started. About a year before I arrived in Tuskegee, some of its black citizens had heard about the Hampton Institute and had applied to their state legislature for a small grant with which to start a

Tuskegee school to train black teachers. In response, the legislature had approved an annual grant of $2,000. This money, however, could be used only to pay the instructors' salaries. There was no grant for land, buildings, or equipment.

Tuskegee's black citizens were very interested in politics and anxious that I share their views. Several times their designated spokesman came to me and said, "We wants you to vote jus' like *we* votes. We can't read de newspapers much, but we knows how to vote. We watches de white men 'til we finds out which way dey's goin' to vote. Den we votes 'xactly de *other* way."

I spent much of my first month in Alabama traveling around the state, especially in the rural areas. I traveled mainly over country roads, in a mule-drawn cart or buggy. I ate and slept with the people, in their little cabins. I saw their farms, schools, and churches. Because most of my visits were unexpected, I saw people's real everyday lives.

I met some interesting people. One black man, who was about sixty years old, said that he had been born in Virginia and sold into Alabama in 1845. I asked him, "How many of you were sold at the same time?" He answered, "Five: me, my brother, and three mules."

In the plantation districts, most families slept in one room, sometimes with non-relatives. More than once, I went outside a cabin to get ready for bed or to wait until the family had gone to bed. Usually I slept on the floor or in someone's bed. Few cabins had any place where people could wash their faces or hands; usually this was done in the yard.

Many cabins had a sewing machine that cost as much as $60 and was being paid off in installments or a showy clock that cost $12 or $14. When I sat down to dinner with one family of four, there was only one fork. Yet this family had an organ for which they were paying $60 in monthly installments. Usually the sewing machine went unused, the clock didn't keep the correct time (in nine out of ten cases, no one in the family could read the time anyway), and no one knew how to play the organ.

The common diet was fatty pork and cornbread. Some people had only cornbread and black-eyed peas cooked in water. The people bought pork and cornmeal at high prices at a store in town, even though the land around their cabins could easily support a wide variety of vegetables. They seemed to plant nothing but cotton, in many cases right up to their cabin door. In the counties that I visited, the crops usually were mortgaged, and most of the black farmers were in debt.

Usually, when the family got up in the morning, the mother would put a piece of meat in one frying pan and a lump of dough in another and place the pans on the fire; breakfast would be ready in ten or fifteen minutes. Frequently the father would take his meat and bread in his hand and start for the field, eating while he walked. The mother would sit down in a corner and eat her breakfast, either from a plate or directly from the frying pans, while her children ate their meat and bread as they ran around the yard. At certain seasons, when meat was scarce, the children who were too young or weak to work in the fields rarely got any meat.

When breakfast was over, the whole family usually would proceed to the cotton field, with practically no attention having been given to the cabin. Every child large enough to carry a hoe was put to work. Babies (there usually was at least one baby) would be laid down at the end of the cotton row, so that their mothers could give them some attention when they finished chopping their rows. Lunch and supper were eaten in much the same way as breakfast.

Every weekday followed pretty much the

same routine. On Saturday the whole family would spend at least half a day in town. Most of this time was spent standing on the streets. The women often sat around smoking or taking snuff. Sunday usually was spent going to some big meeting.

The state hadn't built schoolhouses in the rural areas. As a rule, school was taught in churches or log cabins. During the winter, some houses used as schools might have had no heating. Consequently a fire had to be built in the yard, and teacher and pupils repeatedly went to the fire to get warm. Except for an occasional rough blackboard, there was virtually no equipment in these schoolhouses. In one abandoned cabin being used as a schoolhouse, I found five pupils studying from one book. Two sat with the book between them, two others peeped over their shoulders, and a fifth peeped over the shoulders of the other four.

Most of the teachers in these rural schools were miserably unprepared to teach. The schools were in session only three to five months.

What I saw during my month of travel left me with a heavy heart. What could be done to help the children I had met? I saw more clearly than ever the wisdom of Hampton's system. A few hours of mere book education would be largely a waste of time for the children I had seen. In fact, during my travels one of the saddest things that I saw was a young man, who had attended some high school, sitting in a one-room cabin, with grease on his clothing, filth all around him, and weeds in the yard and garden, studying French grammar.

CHAPTER 8

TEACHING IN A STABLE AND A HENHOUSE

After searching for a suitable location for the Tuskegee Normal and Industrial Institute, I had to settle for a rundown shack, loaned by Tuskegee's citizens, near the town's black Methodist church.

I set July 4, 1881 as the day for the institute's opening. The planned institute generated much discussion among both blacks and whites. Some whites viewed it with disfavor. They questioned its value to blacks and said that it might cause trouble between blacks and whites. Some whites believed that blacks would become less economically useful if they became better educated. They feared that education would cause blacks to leave the farms and would make it more difficult to hire them as servants.

The two men who had written to General Armstrong for a teacher were George Campbell, an ex-slaveholder, and Lewis Adams, an ex-slave. Mr. Campbell was a merchant and banker with little experience related to education. Mr. Adams was a mechanic who had learned shoemaking, harness making, and tinsmithing during slavery. He never had been to school, but he somehow had learned to read and write while a slave. From the first, these two men clearly understood my educational plan and supported me in every effort.

On the morning that the school opened, thirty students reported for admission. Many more students wanted to enter the school, but it had been decided to accept only those who were at least fifteen and had previously received some education. The students were about equally divided between the sexes. Some of them were nearly forty. Most of them lived in the county.

Most were public-school teachers who wanted an education because they thought that it would enable them to earn more money as teachers. With the teachers came some of their former pupils. Upon examination, several of these pupils entered a higher class than their former teachers.

Nearly every registered student had one or

more middle initials. When I asked what the "A" in "John A. Jones" stood for, I was told that this was part of the student's "entitles."

Some of the students had studied big books and claimed to have mastered high-sounding subjects. The bigger the book and the longer the name of the subject, the prouder they felt of their accomplishment. Some had studied Latin, and one or two Greek. They thought that this gave them distinction. While they could locate the Sahara Desert or the capital of China on a globe, or had memorized complicated rules of grammar and math, they had little idea as to how they might apply their knowledge to everyday life. They said they had mastered banking and accounting, but neither they nor most of the other people in their neighborhood had ever had a bank account. I had to tell students who had been studying cube roots that first they should master the multiplication table. I soon learned that most of the students knew only a smattering of the high-sounding things that they had studied.

The number of pupils increased each week. By the end of the first month, there were nearly fifty. However, many of them said that they could remain only two or three months, so they wanted to enter an advanced class and, if possible, get a diploma the first year.

At the end of the first six weeks, Olivia Davidson arrived to be a second teacher. She was from Ohio, where she had attended public school.

When little more than a girl, Olivia heard that the South needed teachers, so she went to Mississippi to teach. One of her Mississippi pupils contracted smallpox. Everyone else in the community was too frightened of the disease to nurse the boy, but Olivia closed her school and remained by his bedside day and night until he recovered.

While she was on vacation at her Ohio home, a yellow fever epidemic broke out in Memphis, Tennessee. Although she had never had the disease, Olivia immediately telegraphed the city's mayor, offering her services as a nurse. She also taught in Memphis.

Olivia's experiences in the South convinced her that blacks needed more than book learning, so she went to Hampton to prepare herself for better work in the South. After she graduated, she decided to attend the Massachusetts State Normal School at Framingham. Before she went, someone suggested that, because she was light-skinned, she might find it more comfortable to "pass" for white in Framingham. Olivia replied that under no circumstances would she deny being black. She completed a two-year course at the Framingham school.

After graduating, she came to Tuskegee, bringing many valuable ideas regarding the best teaching methods. From the first, Olivia and I consulted about the school's future. The students were making good progress in developing their minds, but practical matters needed attention. The students knew little about good hygiene, nutrition, or learning a trade, and Olivia and I considered these matters important.

Most of our students came from rural areas, where agriculture was the main livelihood. About 85 percent of blacks in the Gulf states were farmers. We wanted to give our students an education that would prepare many of them to be teachers, but also encourage them to return to their plantation districts and show blacks there how to improve their farming.

The more that Olivia and I talked with the students, who were then coming to us from several parts of Alabama, the more we found that the chief ambition of many was to get an education so that they wouldn't have to work with their hands anymore. This reminded me of a story about a black Alabama man. One

July day he suddenly stopped his work in a cotton field, looked up at the sky, and said, "Oh Lawd, de cotton is so grassy, de work is so hard, and the sun is so hot dat I b'lieve I's called to preach."

During the first months that I boarded and taught in the shack, it leaked whenever it rained. More than once, my landlady held an umbrella over me while I ate breakfast. During class, one of the students would leave his lessons and hold an umbrella over me while I heard the other students recite.

Our library and reading room were in one corner of the shack. The whole thing occupied a space about five by twelve feet.

About three months after the school opened, an old, abandoned plantation came onto the market. It was about a mile from the town of Tuskegee. The mansion, which had been occupied by its owners during slavery, had been burned. Olivia and I examined the place and thought that it was an excellent location in which to make the school's work more effective and permanent.

The price was $500, cheap for the property. But neither the school nor I had any money. The owner agreed to let the school occupy the place if I would pay $250 right away and the other $250 within a year.

I wrote to General Marshall, explaining the situation and asking if Hampton could lend me $250, for which I would be personally responsible. To my joy and gratitude, he replied that he had no authority to lend me money belonging to Hampton, but he gladly would lend me $250 from his own funds.

I lost no time getting ready to move the school to the new farm, which had a cabin (formerly used as a dining room), an old kitchen, a stable, and an old henhouse. Within a few weeks, the school was using all of these structures. We repaired the stable and used it as a recitation room.

One morning I told an old black man, who lived nearby and sometimes helped me, that the school had grown so large that we needed to use the henhouse. "Will you help me clean it?" I asked. He replied, "What you mean, boss? You surely ain't goin' to clean out de henhouse in de daytime!" In his view, I mustn't be seen doing such dirty, menial work.

The students did most of the work of getting the new location ready, each afternoon after school. As soon as the existing structures were usable, I determined to clear some land for planting. When I explained my plan to the young men, they were not very receptive. It was hard for them to see the connection between clearing land and becoming educated. Also, many of them had been teachers, and they thought that clearing land was beneath their dignity. To relieve them from any embarrassment, each afternoon after school I took my ax and led the way to the woods. When they saw that I was not ashamed to labor, they began to assist with more enthusiasm. We kept at the work each afternoon, until we had cleared about twenty acres and had planted a crop.

Meanwhile, Olivia was arranging ways to repay the loan. She personally canvassed Tuskegee's citizens, asking them to donate a cake, a chicken, bread, pies, or some other item that could be sold at a festival. To my knowledge, not a single black or white family who was asked failed to donate something. We held several festivals and raised quite a sum.

We also canvassed blacks and whites for financial contributions. Most gave small amounts. The contributions from older blacks were especially touching. Sometimes these people gave five cents or twenty-five cents. Sometimes they contributed a quilt or some sugar cane.

One black woman of about seventy years

came to see me when we were raising money to pay for the farm. Leaning on a cane, she hobbled into the room. Her clothes were ragged but clean. She said, "Mr. Washin'ton, God knows I spent de bes' days of my life in slavery. God knows I's ignorant an' poor. But I knows what you an' Miss Davidson is tryin' to do. I knows you is tryin' to make better men an' better women for de colored race. I ain't got no money, but I wants you to take dese six eggs, what I's been savin' up, an' I wants you to put dese six eggs into de edication of dese boys an' gals."

CHAPTER 9

ANXIOUS DAYS, SLEEPLESS NIGHTS

My first Christmas in Alabama gave me further insight into the people's customs. Between 2 a.m. and 5 a.m. on Christmas morning, some fifty children rapped at the school's doors, asking for "Christmas gifts! Christmas gifts!"

Before emancipation, slaveholders generally gave slaves a week off at Christmas. Black men, and often women, were expected to get drunk. Continuing that custom, the blacks around Tuskegee stopped working from the day before Christmas until after New Year's. People who otherwise didn't drink indulged to excess during this week. There was widespread hilarity and a free use of firearms.

During Christmas vacation, I went some distance from the town to visit the blacks on one large plantation. Most had ceased doing fieldwork and were lounging around their homes. One man, a preacher, tried to convince me, based on the story of Adam and Eve in the Garden of Eden, that God had cursed all labor and that, therefore, it was a sin to work. For that reason he sought to do as little work as possible. As he expressed it, during Christmas week he got to live without sin.

In one cabin five children had nothing to remind them of Christmas other than a bunch of firecrackers, which they had divided among themselves. In another cabin at least six people had only ten cents' worth of ginger cakes, which had been bought in the store the day before. Another family had only a few pieces of sugar cane. In another cabin I found nothing but a new jug of cheap whiskey, which the husband and wife were drinking freely, even though the husband was a minister. In a few instances, people had gotten hold of some brightly colored cards, designed for advertising, and were making the most of those. In other homes some family member had bought a new pistol.

At night the people usually had what they called a "frolic" in some cabin on the plantation. A "frolic" was a dance at which there was likely to be much drinking, and there might be some shooting or cutting with razors.

From the first, I resolved to make the school part of the community in which it was located. Asking the citizens to contribute toward the school property helped them to feel that it was *their* school.

After three months of fundraising, the school had the $250 needed to repay General Marshall. Within two more months, we obtained another $250 and received a deed for the farm's hundred acres. This gave us tremendous satisfaction.

Our next goal was to increase the cultivation of the land, as a means of obtaining food, giving the students agricultural training, and giving them a way to earn their board, so that they could stay in school throughout the nine-month academic year. A white resident of Tuskegee gave the school its first farm animal: an old, blind horse.

School enrollment continued to grow, so we turned our attention to providing a large, substantial building. We had plans drawn for a building, which we decided to name Porter Hall (after a benefactor). The building's estimated cost was $6,000.

When word of the planned building spread around town, a white man who operated a nearby sawmill came to me and said that he gladly would provide all the lumber needed to erect the building, with no guarantee of payment other than my word that we would pay for the lumber when we could. I told the man that we didn't have a single dollar of the needed money. Nevertheless, he insisted on providing the lumber. After the school raised some of the needed funds, I agreed.

Olivia resumed fundraising among blacks and whites. An old black man traveled twelve miles to one fundraising meeting, with a large pig in his ox cart. During the meeting he rose and said that he had no money, but that he had brought one of the two fine pigs that he had raised. He ended his announcement by saying, "Any man here that's got any love for his race, or any respect for himself, will bring a pig to the next meeting." Quite a few men also volunteered to give several days' work toward erecting the building.

Olivia went North to obtain additional funds. On her boat trip, she conversed with a New York woman who became so interested in Tuskegee that she donated $50. For weeks Olivia visited individuals and spoke in churches, before other organizations, and before Sunday schools. She found this work trying and often embarrassing, but she was quite successful.

The students began digging out the earth where Porter Hall's foundations would be laid. They had not fully outgrown the idea that it was improper for them to do manual labor. As some of them expressed it, they had come to Tuskegee "to be educated, not to work." Gradually, though, a desire to work gained ground. After a few weeks of hard work, the foundations were ready, and a day was appointed for the laying of the cornerstone.

When the cornerstone was laid, only sixteen years had passed since the abolition of slavery. Only sixteen years earlier in that part of the country, no black could be taught from books without the teacher being condemned by law and public sentiment. Among those attending the ceremony were prominent whites and many blacks whom they once had held as property.

I was determined to have Tuskegee's buildings built by the students themselves. Most of our students came to us in poverty, from the cabins of cotton, sugar, and rice plantations. I felt that building the school themselves would give them valuable self-reliance and skills, from brick making and masonry to blacksmithing, carpentry, and architecture.

While we were building Porter Hall, the need for money became urgent. I had given one of our creditors a promise that on a certain day, he would be paid $400. On the morning of that day we did not have a single dollar. The mail arrived at the school at 10 a.m., and it included a check, from two Boston women, for exactly $400!

Before Porter Hall was completed, we passed through some very trying seasons. More than once, bills came due that we were unable to pay. Night after night I rolled and tossed—sleepless—in my bed because of anxiety over our financial situation. However, throughout our difficulties I never appealed to a white or black in the town of Tuskegee who did not help according to his means.

CHAPTER 10

MAKING BRICKS

In the school's early days, I think that my most trying experience was brick making. We needed bricks for our own buildings, but there was another reason to establish this skill: the town had no brickyard, so there was a market for bricks.

We tried several locations before we opened up a pit that furnished brick clay. I had always supposed that brick making was simple, but I soon found that it required special skill and knowledge, particularly in the burning of the bricks. After considerable effort we molded about twenty-five thousand bricks and put them into a kiln to be burned. The kiln failed because it was improperly constructed. We began at once on a second kiln. This, too, failed. Several teachers who had been trained at Hampton volunteered their services, and we constructed a third kiln. Burning bricks required about a week. Toward the end of the week, when it seemed we were going to have thousands of bricks within a few hours, the kiln collapsed in the middle of the night.

The failure of the third kiln left me without a single dollar for another attempt. Most of the teachers thought that I should abandon the idea of making bricks. I went to the nearby city of Montgomery and pawned my watch for $15. Then I returned to Tuskegee and, with the help of the $15, rallied our demoralized forces and began a fourth attempt to make bricks. This time we succeeded. (I never have regretted the loss of my watch.)

Many whites who had had no contact (and perhaps no sympathy) with the school came to us to buy bricks because they learned that ours were of good quality. We got acquainted with them, and they traded with us. Our business interests became intermingled.

Brick making was hard and dirty, so it was difficult to get the students to help. It was not a pleasant task to stand in a mud pit for hours, with mud up to your knees. More than one student became disgusted and left the school.

Students also built wagons, carts, and buggies. Increasingly, however, they objected to manual labor.

By this time it was widely known that all Tuskegee students, whatever their financial situation, must learn a trade. Quite a few parents sent letters protesting against their children engaging in labor while at the school. Other parents came to the school and protested in person. Most new students brought a written or verbal request from their parents that they should be taught nothing but books.

I traveled around the state, speaking to parents and trying to convince them of the value of vocational education. I also continually talked to the students about the subject.

In summer 1882, at the end of the school's first year, I went North to raise funds. The first town I went to was Northampton, Massachusetts. Assuming that no hotel would admit me, I spent nearly half a day looking for a black family with whom I could board. I was greatly surprised when I found that I would have no trouble being accommodated at a hotel.

That same summer, I married Fannie Smith. Fannie was from Malden and a graduate of Hampton. In the fall Fannie and I began keeping house in Tuskegee. This provided a home for our teachers, who now numbered four.

Notwithstanding the unpopularity of manual work, the school continued to grow. By the middle of the second year, attendance was about 150, with students from nearly all parts of Alabama and a few students from other states.

Porter Hall was near enough to completion that we felt we could provide meals in part of it. The students helped to dig out a basement. Within a few weeks, we were using the basement as a kitchen and dining room, but it was damp and poorly lit. At first we cooked outdoors, in pots and pans over a fire, because we had no stove. We used some carpenter's benches—previously used in constructing Porter Hall—as tables. We had few dishes.

For the first two weeks something was wrong at every meal. The meat was undercooked or burned, or the salt had been left out of the bread, or the tea had been forgotten.

One morning when the entire breakfast had been a failure, I was standing near the dining room door and heard many student complaints. A young woman who had failed to get any breakfast came out to draw some water from the well. When she reached the well, she found that the rope was broken. She couldn't get any water. Not knowing that I was within hearing, she turned from the well and said, in the most discouraged tone, "We can't even get water to drink at this school."

Another time, a trustee who was visiting the school and who had been given a bedroom over the dining room was awakened early in the morning by an argument between two boys in the dining room. They were disputing whose turn it was to use the coffee cup. One boy won the dispute by proving that he hadn't had any chance to use the cup for three mornings in a row.

CHAPTER
11

MAKING YOUR BED
BEFORE YOU LIE IN IT

When we opened our boarding department, we provided attic rooms in Porter Hall
for a number of young women and found
rooms outside the school grounds for many of
the young men. We charged the students $8 a
month for room and board. We gave them
credit against their bills for work that they did
at the school. Fundraising covered each student's tuition, which was $50 a year.

To provide further sleeping accommodations, we rented a number of cabins near the
school. These cabins were rundown. In winter the boys who occupied them suffered
from the cold. We were not able to provide
enough bed clothes to keep them warm.

In fact, for some time we were able to

provide only a few bedsteads and mattresses. Students were expected, as far as possible, to make their own furniture. They patiently slept on the floor until a bedstead was built and went without a mattress until one was made. Very few students had any carpentry skills, so the student-made bedsteads were rough and weak. Not infrequently, when I went into the students' rooms in the morning, I would find at least two bedsteads lying about on the floor. We finally solved the problem of providing mattresses by sewing pieces of cheap cloth into large bags and filling these bags with pine needles from nearby forests.

Initially we had no chairs in the bedrooms or dining room. The students made stools by nailing together three pieces of rough board. As a rule, the furniture in the students' rooms consisted of a bed, some stools, and sometimes a student-made table.

During the coldest nights I was so troubled about the discomfort of the boys in the cabins that I couldn't sleep. On several occasions I went to their cabins, in the middle of the night, to comfort them. I found some of them sitting huddled around a fire, with the one blanket that we had been able to provide wrapped around them. Some of them didn't attempt to lie down the entire night. One morning, after an especially cold night, I asked the students who were in the chapel if any of them thought they been frostbitten during the night. Three raised their hands.

Even before there was any kind of bathhouse, we started teaching the students to bathe regularly. Most of them came from plantation districts. Often we had to teach them how to sleep with two sheets (after we could *provide* them with two sheets). For a long time, one of the most difficult lessons was that their clothes must have no tears, grease spots, or missing buttons.

As the number of students continued to increase, we decided to construct a larger building, Alabama Hall, with rooms for girls and meal accommodations for both boys and girls. We estimated that this building would cost about $10,000. Again we worked at fundraising. Again the students began to dig so that foundations could be laid.

At this time I received a telegram from General Armstrong asking me if I could come to Hampton right away and spend a month traveling with him through the North. I left immediately. Upon arriving at Hampton, I learned that General Armstrong had decided to take a quartet of singers through the North and hold meetings in major cities. He and I would speak at these meetings, which would benefit Tuskegee. Hampton would cover all expenses. The trip raised much-needed funds for Alabama Hall.

In 1884 Tuskegee established a night school to accommodate some students too poor to pay even the small charges at Tuskegee. Initially, about a dozen students attended. The night school was organized on a plan similar to the one that I had helped to establish at Hampton: students were required to work at some trade for ten hours during the day and to study academic subjects for two hours during the evening; they were paid more than the cost of their board, with most of their earnings being reserved in the school's treasury toward their future board in the regular day school. After one or two years, night-school students would enter the day school, where they would study academic subjects four days a week and work at a trade two days a week.

CHAPTER 12

BIRTH AND DEATH

Fannie and I had one daughter, Portia. In 1884, after devoted work for Tuskegee, Fannie died.

In 1885 Olivia and I married. She divided her time between our home, work for the institute, and community work. She taught at the institute, was its Lady Principal, taught a Sunday school class in the town of Tuskegee, and worked among older people in and around the town. She also continued to fundraise in the North and South, through personal visits and correspondence. Many nights, after spending the day going door to door trying to interest people in the institute's work, she was too exhausted to undress herself. Once, she called on a Boston woman who couldn't see her right away. Olivia waited in the woman's parlor. When the woman entered the parlor, she found Olivia asleep.

Olivia and I had two bright, beautiful sons: Booker Taliaferro and Ernest Davidson. In 1889, after four years of happy married life and eight years of hard but happy work for the school, Olivia died. She literally had worn herself out in her ceaseless efforts.

In 1893 I married Margaret Murray, a native of Mississippi and a graduate of Fisk University. Margaret had come to Tuskegee as a teacher several years before. At the time we married, she was Lady Principal.

CHAPTER 13

MY ATLANTA SPEECH

In 1895 plans were underway for the Atlanta Cotton States and International Exposition, to be held in Atlanta, Georgia on September 18. The exposition would include a Negro Building—wholly designed and built by blacks—devoted to showing the progress of blacks since emancipation. This building would include exhibits on Hampton and Tuskegee.

The exposition's board of directors invited me to give one of the event's opening speeches. To my knowledge, this was the first time that any black had been asked to speak from the same platform as white Southerners at a national event. Northern and Southern newspapers discussed my coming speech. Some Southern white papers objected to my speaking.

On the morning of September 17, my family started for Atlanta. I would be speaking to blacks, Southern whites, and Northern whites. When I got off the train in Atlanta, an old black man said, "Dat's de man of my race what's goin' to make a speech at de exposition tomorrow. I's sure goin' to hear him."

Atlanta was packed with people from all parts of the country and with representatives of foreign governments. The afternoon papers' headlines advertised the next day's proceedings. I didn't sleep much that night.

Early in the morning, a committee called to escort me to my place in the procession that would march to the exposition grounds. This procession included prominent black citizens in carriages, as well as representatives of several black military organizations. The procession took about three hours to reach the exposition grounds. Throughout that time, the sun was intensely hot. By the time we reached the grounds, the heat and my nervousness had combined to make me feel ready to collapse.

When I entered the large auditorium, it was packed with people. Loud cheers came from the black section of the audience, and fainter cheers from some whites. While in Atlanta, I had been told that some whites in the audience would be in sympathy with me, some others would be there only out of curiosity, and many would be there to hear me make a fool of myself, after which they would be able to tell the officials who had invited me, "I told you so!"

My friend William Baldwin, a Tuskegee trustee and general manager of the Southern Railroad, was in Atlanta that day. He was so nervous about the kind of reception that I would receive, and the effect that my speech would produce, that he couldn't bring himself to enter the building. Instead he walked back and forth outside until the opening exercises ended.

The exposition opened with a short address from Governor Bullock of Georgia. After some other presentations and speeches, he introduced me as "a representative of Negro enterprise and Negro civilization."

When I rose to speak, there was considerable cheering, especially from the black members of the audience. Thousands of people were looking intently into my face.

I opened by saying that one-third of the South's population was black. I urged blacks to acquire property, as well as agricultural, industrial, and business skills. I said that blacks would prosper to the extent that we learned to "dignify and glorify common labor," "put brains and skill into the common occupations of life," and distinguish useless, superficial things from useful, substantial ones. I commented that "there is as much dignity in tilling a field as in writing a poem." I said that because blacks had been slaves, we were forced to start "at the bottom." But we shouldn't let our grievances "overshadow our opportunities." I said that society should make every effort to develop black skill and intelligence, not restrict them. When blacks were emancipated, I said, we owned only "a few quilts and pumpkins and chickens." Now we had produced agricultural tools, steam engines, newspapers, books, statues, and paintings. We managed drugstores and banks. "It is important and right that all privileges of the law be ours," I said, but blacks must prepare themselves to exercise those privileges. I called for friendship between blacks and whites.

When my speech ended, Governor Bullock rushed across the platform and shook my hand. Others did the same. I received so many hearty congratulations that I found it difficult to leave the building.

The next morning I went into Atlanta's business district. As soon as I was recognized, a crowd of men surrounded me and wanted to shake my hand.

Newspapers in all parts of the country published the full text of my speech. For months after, editorials complimented it.

At first, black newspapers and black citizens seemed greatly pleased with my Atlanta speech. However, after the first burst of enthusiasm, many blacks expressed the view that I had been too generous in my remarks about Southern whites and had not spoken out strongly enough for black rights.

I received numerous offers to give lectures and write newspaper and magazine articles. One lecture bureau offered me $50,000, or $200 a night plus expenses, if I would place my services at their disposal for a given period. I declined all such offers, saying that my life's work was at Tuskegee and that whenever I spoke, it must be to advance Tuskegee or the well-being of blacks, not for my own profit.

To the extent that I could spare the time from immediate work at Tuskegee, I accepted public-speaking invitations, especially those that would take me into territory where I thought it would pay to plead the cause of blacks. I have spoken, among other places, at men's and women's clubs, church meetings, professional societies, business organizations, universities, and national events. Some people who have shaken my hand after one of my speeches have said that they never before called a black man "Mister."

CHAPTER 14

PLEASANT SURPRISES

In 1896, while I was sitting on the veranda of my home at Tuskegee, surrounded by Margaret and the children, I received the greatest surprise of my life: a letter informing me that Harvard University wished to give me an honorary degree. Tears came into my eyes. My whole former life passed before me: my experiences as a plantation slave, my work in the coal mine, the times when I was without food and clothing, the time that I slept under a boardwalk, my struggles for an education, the trying days at Tuskegee when I did not know where to turn for financial support.

In June I attended Harvard's graduation ceremony. Among the others there to receive an honorary degree was Alexander Graham Bell, inventor of the telephone. When my name was called, I rose, and Harvard's president conferred upon me the degree of Master of Arts.

This was the first time that a New England university had conferred an honorary degree on a black. An editorial in a Boston newspaper stated, "In conferring the honorary degree of Master of Arts upon the Principal of Tuskegee Institute, Harvard University has honored itself as well as the object of this distinction. The work which Professor Booker T. Washington has accomplished for the education, good citizenship, and popular enlightenment in his chosen field of labor in the South entitles him to rank with our national benefactors."

In spring 1899, some Boston women arranged a public meeting to benefit Tuskegee. Many of Boston's leading citizens, both black and white, attended. I gave a speech, Paul Lawrence Dunbar read from his poems, and W.E.B. Du Bois read an original literary piece.

Some attendees noticed that I seemed unusually tired. Soon after the meeting ended, a woman asked me if I ever had been to Europe. I said no. A few days later I was informed that some Boston friends had raised money for Margaret and me to visit Europe for three months.

I was taken completely by surprise. For

eighteen years I had worked steadily in connection with Tuskegee. I thanked my Boston friends for their thoughtfulness and generosity, but said that I couldn't leave the school because it couldn't survive financially in my absence. They then informed me that the sum being raised would suffice to keep the school running while I was away.

I always had wanted to go to Europe. At the same time, I feared that people would not know the full circumstances of my vacation and might think that Margaret and I were being self-indulgent. Also, it seemed selfish of me to take a vacation while others remained hard at work and so much needed to be done.

Finally, Margaret and I agreed to go. Our Boston friends mapped out our route, gave us letters of introduction to people in France and England, and made other arrangements for our trip.

In May, Margaret and I boarded a large, beautiful steamer in New York. When the steamer left the wharf, the load of anxiety and responsibility that I had carried for eighteen years began to fall from my shoulders at the rate of a pound a minute.

Margaret and I had one of the most comfortable rooms on the ship. The second or third day out, I began to sleep. I think that I slept fifteen hours a day during the remainder of the ten days' voyage.

After ten days of delightful weather, during which I never was seasick, we landed at Antwerp, Belgium. The next day was bright and beautiful. Our hotel room faced the main public square. We saw people come in from the countryside with brightly polished cans of milk and all kinds of beautiful flowers to sell. People streamed into the cathedral.

After spending some time in Antwerp, we were invited to join six other people on a trip through Holland. The group included some Americans who had come over on the steamer with us. We enjoyed the trip greatly. Most of the way, we traveled on a slow, old-fashioned canal boat. I was greatly impressed with Holland's agriculture. I never had realized how much people could get out of a small plot of ground.

From Holland we returned to Belgium. We made a hasty trip through that country, stopping at Brussels.

Next we went to Paris, where Theodore Stanton, the son of Elizabeth Cady Stanton, kindly provided accommodations for us. We had barely gotten settled in Paris when I was invited to speak at a University Club of Paris banquet. The other guests at the banquet included ex-President Benjamin Harrison, who spoke much of Tuskegee's work and my own efforts. After my banquet speech, I received other invitations but declined most of them. I still was catching up on my sleep.

While in Paris, Margaret and I saw much of the black painter Henry Tanner, whom we had known in America. When we told some Americans that we were going to the Luxembourg Palace to see a Tanner painting, they found it hard to believe that the work of a black was displayed there. I think they weren't convinced until they saw the picture for themselves.

From Paris, Margaret and I went to London. Friends had provided us with numerous letters of introduction and had informed other people of our coming. Margaret and I were flooded with invitations to attend social functions, and many of the invitations asked me to give a speech. As in Paris, I declined most of the invitations because I wanted to rest. However, I did speak at a public meeting attended by many people, including several members of Parliament. Also, the U.S. Ambassador gave a reception for Margaret and me. There, for the first time, I met Mark Twain.

In Birmingham, England, Margaret and I

were the guests for several days of Joseph Sturge, whose father was a great abolitionist and friend of James G. Whittier and William Lloyd Garrison. Throughout England it was a great privilege to meet people who had known Garrison, Frederick Douglass, and other abolitionists. The English abolitionists we met seemed never to tire of talking about Garrison and Douglass. Before going to England, I hadn't realized how deeply interested English abolitionists had been in the cause of freedom for black Americans, and how much help they had given.

Some attendees of the International Congress of Women, which was in session in London, invited Margaret and me to accompany them to Windsor Castle, where we all had tea with Queen Victoria. Susan B. Anthony was among our group.

At the House of Commons, which we visited several times, we met Henry M. Stanley. I talked with him about Africa and its relation to American blacks. After our discussion, I was more convinced than ever that there was no hope of American blacks improving their condition by emigrating to Africa.

After three months in Europe, we sailed from Southampton, England, on the steamship *St. Louis*. The steamer had a fine library. I found an autobiography of Frederick Douglass, which I began reading. In his book Douglass described how he was treated on a ship during his first or second visit to England. He was not permitted to enter the ship's cabin but had to stay on the deck.

How strongly my shipboard experience contrasted with that of Douglass! A few minutes after I finished reading about *his*, a committee of men and women requested that I deliver an address at a concert to be given the following evening. After the concert, some passengers proposed that a subscription be raised to help the work at Tuskegee. Enough money for several scholarships resulted.

In addition to Tuskegee's work, I felt that nationwide networks of blacks were enormously important. In summer 1900, with the assistance of other blacks, I organized the National Negro Business League, which held its first meeting in Boston and brought together for the first time many blacks engaged in various trades and businesses in different parts of the United States. Thirty states were represented at our first meeting. State and local business leagues grew out of this national meeting.

Nine years before, I had organized the first Negro Conference. This is now an annual gathering that brings eight or nine hundred black men and women to Tuskegee. Conference attendees spend a day learning about the needs of blacks and planning how to meet those needs. Numerous state and local conferences doing the same kind of work have grown out of Tuskegee's central Negro Conference.

CHAPTER 15

TUSKEGEE IN 1901

Twenty years have passed since I began my work at Tuskegee, in a broken-down shack. Back then, the institute owned no property. It had one teacher and thirty students.

Today Tuskegee's students number 1,400 and come from dozens of states, Puerto Rico, Jamaica, Cuba, Africa, and other countries. The night school has 457 students. Tuskegee is so popular that we have to turn away half of those who apply for admission. This is true even though the school's regimen remains highly rigorous and demanding:

5:00 a.m.: rising bell
6:00: breakfast
6:20: room cleaning
6:50: work
7:30: study
8.25: inspection of young men's clothing and grooming

8:40: chapel services
8:55: daily news
9:00: classes
noon: break
12:15 p.m.: lunch
1:00: work
1:30: classes
3:30: work
5:30: break
6:00: supper
7:10: prayers
7:30: study
8:45: break
9:30: bedtime

At Tuskegee we continue to stress personal hygiene. Several times in recent years, students have come to Tuskegee with almost nothing except a toothbrush. They have heard from older students that we insist on tooth brushing. One morning not long ago, I accompanied the Lady Principal on her morning inspection of the girls' rooms. One room was occupied by three girls who had recently arrived at the school. When I asked them if they had toothbrushes, one of the girls pointed to a brush and said, "Yes, sir. That is our brush. We bought it together, yesterday." They quickly learned a different lesson.

Tuskegee now owns 2,300 acres of land.

Each year, 1,000 of these acres are under cultivation, entirely by student labor. One of our graduates produced 266 bushels of sweet potatoes from one acre of ground in a community where the average production was only 49 bushels per acre. He was able to do this because of his knowledge of soil chemistry and of improved agricultural methods. Tuskegee students learn a wide range of agricultural skills, including gardening and fruit growing.

Former students often return to Tuskegee. They go into our large, beautiful dining room and see tempting, well-cooked food, largely grown by the students themselves. They see tables with neat tablecloths, napkins, and vases of flowers. Often they tell me that they are glad that we started as we did—that we built ourselves up, year after year, by a slow, natural process of growth.

The school currently has sixty-six buildings. All but four of them were built almost entirely by students. Not a few times, when a new student has been tempted to mar some building with pencil marks or knife cuts, I have heard an older student say, "Don't do that. That's *our* building. I helped put it up."

Tuskegee's farm uses dozens of wagons, carts, and buggies. Students built every one of them. The school also supplies vehicles to the local market.

Tuskegee students still make their own furniture, but the number of pieces in a room has increased, and the furniture is now of the highest quality. The mattresses made by the institute's students are good enough to be sold in stores.

Brick making is an important industry at the school. Last season our students manufactured 1,200,000 first-class bricks. Throughout the South, scores of our graduates are engaged in brick making.

Tuskegee has thirty industrial departments; they teach trades in which our students can find employment as soon as they graduate. The demand for our graduates is so great that we cannot fill half of the requests that we receive for their services.

Although Tuskegee is non-denominational, it includes the Phelps Hall Bible Training School, which prepares students for the ministry and other forms of Christian work, especially work in rural districts. We try to teach *all* of our students to attend to the comfort and happiness of others, especially the unfortunate. Not long ago some of our young men spent the Christmas holiday rebuilding a cabin for an elderly black woman. Another time, I announced that a very poor student was suffering from cold because he needed a coat. The next morning two coats were sent to my office for him.

CHAPTER 16

LAST WORDS

In addition to working for the institute, Margaret runs a mothers' meeting in the town of Tuskegee and assists people who live in a settlement connected with a large plantation about eight miles from Tuskegee. She also is largely responsible for a women's club that meets twice a month to discuss important issues, is president of the Federation of Southern Colored Women's Clubs, and heads the executive committee of the National Federation of Colored Women's Clubs.

Portia has learned dressmaking and has unusual ability in instrumental music. She already teaches at Tuskegee.

Booker has developed great skill in brick masonry, which he began studying when he was quite small. He wants to be an architect and mason.

Ernest plans to be a physician. In addition to going to school, where he studies books and manual skills, he regularly spends part of his time in the office of Tuskegee's resident physician. Ernest already has learned to perform many of the duties associated with a doctor's office.

My brother John is Superintendent of Industries at Tuskegee. Our adopted brother, James, is the institute's postmaster.

I still am Tuskegee's president and principal. As a rule, each day before I leave my office, I clear my desk of all letters and memos, so that the next day I can begin afresh. However, when I have an unusually difficult question to decide, especially one about which I feel much emotion, I find it best to "sleep on it" or wait until I have had a chance to discuss it with Margaret.

My love of reading has stayed with me. Newspapers are a constant source of delight and recreation to me. I also especially enjoy biographies. I like to read about an actual person or thing. I think that I've read nearly every book and magazine article on Abraham Lincoln. My favorite time of day is after the evening meal, when I sit with Margaret and my children and we read a story or take turns telling one.

I also especially enjoy Sunday afternoons when, for an hour or more, we go into the woods, where we are surrounded by pure air, trees, shrubbery, flowers, the chirping of crickets, and the singing of birds. My garden is another source of rest and enjoyment. I like to spend thirty or forty minutes spading the ground, planting seeds, or digging around the plants. I also take much pleasure in raising pigs and fowl. I think that the pig is my favorite animal.

As I write the closing words of this autobiography, I find myself in Richmond, Virginia. Only a few decades ago, that city was the capital of the Confederacy. About twenty-five years ago, I arrived there in such poverty that I slept under a boardwalk. Now I am in Richmond as the guest of the city's black citizens. Last night I delivered a speech, to both blacks and whites, in the Academy of Music, not far from the boardwalk under which I slept. It was the first time that blacks ever had been permitted to use that auditorium. The Virginia legislature attended—the legislature of the state in which I was born into slavery.

AFTERWORD

ABOUT THE AUTHOR

Booker Taliaferro Washington was born a slave in Franklin County, Virginia in 1856. Along with his mother Jane and brother John, he belonged to James Burroughs, who owned a plantation where Jane was the cook. Washington never learned the identity of his father, who was white. While Washington was a small child, Jane married another slave, Washington Ferguson. Jane and Washington had a daughter, Amanda. During the Civil War, Washington Ferguson escaped to West Virginia.

Until Booker T. Washington was nine, his family lived in a small, one-room cabin on Burroughs's plantation. The cabin's windows were holes without glass, the floor was bare earth, and the "stove" was a fireplace. The "bed" that Washington shared with John and Amanda was a pile of rags. His scant clothes consisted of uncomfortable shoes with wooden soles and a flaxen shirt so rough that it scratched his skin. His childhood duties included cleaning yards, carrying water to field slaves, bringing corn to a mill for grinding, and fanning flies away from the Burroughses' dining table at mealtime. Like most other slaves, Washington was denied any schooling.

When the Civil War ended in 1865, all slaves were freed. To join his stepfather, Washington and his family walked most of the distance to Malden, West Virginia. Although Washington was only nine, he went to work at a salt furnace, where he packed newly mined salt into barrels. From ages ten to twelve, he worked as a coal miner. While working, he started teaching himself to read and write and received school lessons part-time, mostly at night.

One day in the coal mine, Washington overheard a man describe the Hampton Normal and Agricultural Institute, a Virginia college where blacks could earn their bed and board while learning a trade. He determined to go to Hampton. In 1872, at age sixteen, he journeyed hundreds of miles to Hampton, often by hitching a ride or walking.

At Hampton, Washington paid his way by

working as a janitor. In addition to academic subjects, he studied agriculture, which included working in the fields and tending pigs. He graduated, with honors, at the age of nineteen.

Booker T. Washington returned to Malden, where he became the teacher and superintendent of a school for black children and adults. In 1879 he accepted a position as a Hampton instructor.

Two years later, Washington became the head of a newly founded teachers' college for blacks: the Tuskegee Normal and Industrial Institute (now Tuskegee University), in Alabama. Washington taught the first classes in a rundown shack that leaked when it rained.

A strong believer in networking, Washington organized the first Negro Conference, at which attendees discussed ways to improve the lives of blacks. He also founded the National Negro Business League, which assisted black business owners.

In 1895 Washington gave a now-famous speech at a world's fair held in Atlanta; from then on, he was in great demand as a public speaker. The next year, he received an honorary master's degree from Harvard University.

Booker T. Washington became one of America's most politically powerful blacks.

U.S. Presidents—Grover Cleveland, William McKinley, Theodore Roosevelt, and William Howard Taft—sought his advice regarding which blacks to appoint to government office.

Washington wrote dozens of books, including The Future of the American Negro (1899), Character Building (1902), The Story of the Negro (1909), and My Larger Education (1911). His autobiography Up from Slavery (1901) is his best-known work.

Washington was married three times: in 1882 to Fannie Smith, who died in 1884; in 1885 to Olivia Davidson, who died in 1889; and in 1893 to Margaret Murray. Fannie was a Hampton graduate from Malden; both Olivia and Margaret taught at Tuskegee and served as the school's vice principal. Washington had a daughter by Fannie and two sons by Olivia.

Until his death in 1915, Booker T. Washington continued as Tuskegee's principal and president. Today numerous schools bear his name, and his birthplace is a national monument. He is regarded as one of the most influential blacks in American history.

ABOUT THE BOOK

Up from Slavery (1901) is, first of all, a success story. Booker T. Washington tells how, through education, he transformed his own life and that of many others. "From the time that I can remember having any thoughts about anything, I had felt an intense desire to learn to read," he writes. "When I was a small child, I decided that, if I accomplished nothing else in life, I somehow would get enough education to be able to read common books and newspapers." Washington far surpasses that modest goal, ending up a world-renowned educator, speaker, and author.

But *Up from Slavery* is also a penetrating glimpse into the mind and heart of a remarkable man. As Washington tells the story of his life, he also reveals his character. He shows us, through vivid examples, the values by which he lived and which helped him to reach and surpass his goals.

In the early chapters of his autobiography, Washington reveals one of his strongest character traits: determination. Until he is nine, Washington is a slave who, like most slaves, receives no schooling. After emancipation, he is permitted to go to school, but his family is so poor that Washington cannot attend school on a regular basis. He works during the day and learns to read and write at night: "Often I had to walk several miles at night to have lessons." He comments, "Throughout my youth, no matter how discouraging my circumstances were, I remained determined to obtain an education."

At age sixteen, Washington is so determined to attend the Hampton Institute—hundreds of miles from his West Virginia home—that he sets out with almost no money. Forced to travel much of the distance on foot, he suffers from cold, hunger, and exhaustion. But after walking long distances, begging rides in wagons, sleeping under boardwalks, and interrupting his trip to do manual labor on a cargo ship, Washington reaches Hampton—with fifty cents in his pocket.

Washington's willingness to work hard, even at menial jobs, is another admirable characteristic. While still a child, he works as a salt packer, then a coal miner, then a house servant, to help provide for his family. After reaching Hampton Institute, he pays his way by working as a janitor. "I had to care for many rooms and work late into the night," he writes. "In addition, I had to rise by 4 a.m. to build the fires and have some time to prepare my lessons." His last year at Hampton, Washington spends "nearly every minute" studying or doing janitorial work. Despite having to work as many hours as he studies, Washington makes the honor roll and graduates at age nineteen.

After graduation, Washington continues to work hard. Because he considers education so essential to black progress, Washington becomes a tireless educator. "So many of Malden's adults and older children had to work during the day, but craved education, that I soon opened a night school. From the first the night school was crowded, about as well attended as the school that I taught during the day. . . . On Sundays I taught two Sunday schools. . . . In addition, I gave private lessons to several young men whom I was preparing for Hampton. Without regard to pay, I taught anyone who wanted to learn anything that I could teach."

Washington's most obvious character trait is his lifelong devotion to education and the benefits it could bring his people. He writes: "Blacks were eager for an education. Few were too young or old to attempt to learn. As fast as teachers could be obtained, day schools and night schools were filled." To

Washington, the economic, social, and political struggle of American blacks largely was the struggle to obtain an education. "Hampton's several hundred students were tremendously in earnest. They spent every hour studying or working. . . . Besides having to wrestle with their books, many of the students were so poor that they had to struggle for life's necessities. Many had elderly parents who were dependent on them; some were married men who had to support their wives."

After beginning his teaching career in Malden, Washington goes on to teach at Hampton. Finally, he becomes the head of the newly founded Tuskegee Institute. In Tuskegee and surrounding areas, he again finds blacks eager to learn. In one rural schoolhouse, he sees "five pupils studying from one book. Two sat with the book between them, two others peeped over their shoulders, and a fifth peeped over the shoulders of the other four."

To Washington, education means more than book learning; it also involves building practical skills and moral character: "A few hours of mere book education would be largely a waste of time for the children I had seen. In fact, during my travels one of the saddest things that I saw was a young man, who had attended some high school, sitting in a one-room cabin, with grease on his clothing, filth all around him, and weeds in the yard and garden, studying French grammar." In Washington's view, knowledge is worth little unless it can be applied to everyday life. He believes that a full education includes every-thing from personal hygiene and good nutri-tion to learning a trade. This is the kind of education that he provides at Tuskegee. While studying academic subjects, the students mas-ter trades such as carpentry, brick making, and farming. In doing so, they learn to take pride in the work they accomplish themselves.

Up from Slavery is the story of a self-made person whose strengths of character help him overcome poverty and oppression. However, as much as Washington himself, the book's hero is education, which leads Washington to goals achieved and dreams fulfilled.

If you liked
Up from Slavery: An Autobiography,
you might be interested in other
books in the Townsend Library.

(continued on following pages)

Harriet Jacobs

Incidents in the Life of a
Slave Girl

Written by Herself

TP THE TOWNSEND LIBRARY

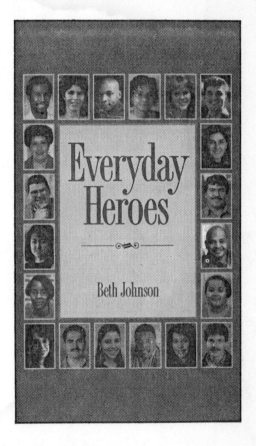

Everyday Heroes

Beth Johnson

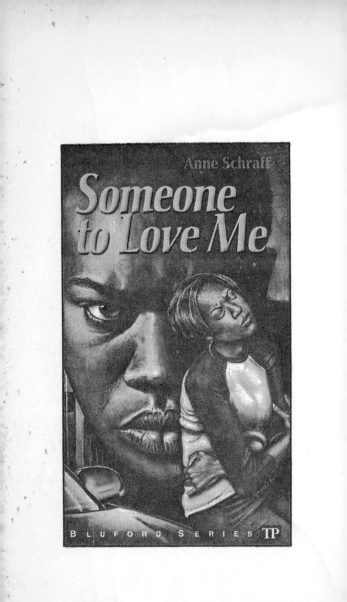

BLUFORD SERIES TP

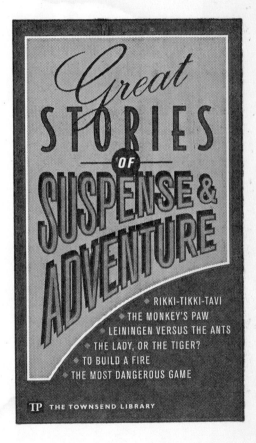

Great STORIES OF SUSPENSE & ADVENTURE

- RIKKI-TIKKI-TAVI
- THE MONKEY'S PAW
- LEININGEN VERSUS THE ANTS
- THE LADY, OR THE TIGER?
- TO BUILD A FIRE
- THE MOST DANGEROUS GAME

TP THE TOWNSEND LIBRARY

READING
CHANGED MY LIFE!

THREE
TRUE
STORIES

Beth Johnson

THE TOWNSEND LIBRARY TP

For more information, visit us at
www.townsendpress.com